CHINOOK & CHANTERELLE

Books *by* ROBERT MICHAEL PYLE

PROSE

Wintergreen: Rambles in a Ravaged Land

The Thunder Tree: Lessons from an Urban Wildland

Where Bigfoot Walks: Crossing the Dark Divide

Nabokov's Butterflies (Editor, with Brian Boyd & Dmitri Nabokov)

Chasing Monarchs: Migrating with the Butterflies of Passage

Walking the High Ridge: Life as Field Trip

Sky Time in Gray's River: Living for Keeps in a Forgotten Place

Mariposa Road: The First Butterfly Big Year

The Tangled Bank: Essays from Orion

POETRY

Letting the Flies Out (chapbook)

Evolution of the Genus Iris

ON ENTOMOLOGY

Watching Washington Butterflies

The Audubon Society Field Guide to North American Butterflies

The IUCN Invertebrate Red Data Book (with S. M. Wells & N. M. Collins)

Handbook for Butterfly Watchers

Butterflies: A Peterson Field Guide Coloring Book (with Roger Tory Peterson & Sarah Anne Hughes)

Insects: A Peterson Field Guide Coloring Book (with Kristin Kest)

The Butterflies of Cascadia

CHINOOK & CHANTERELLE

Robert Michael Pyle

poems

LOST HORSE PRESS
Sandpoint, Idaho

ACKNOWLEDGMENTS

Adventures NW: "Danke Schoen" & "In Sequoia, in 1969"
Alaska Quarterly Review: "Out of Its Element"
A Voice for the Earth: American Writers Respond to the Earth Charter: "Who?"
Camas: "City of Rocks"
Honoring Our Rivers: "Platypus Becomes One With Water"
Letting the Flies Out: "The Watermelon" & "Upon Obtaining My Golden Eagle Pass"
Northwest Coast: "Chinook and Chanterelle"
Outposted: "Girl, Book, Brook"
Outpost 2015: "The Shriving of the Swallows" & "Unintended Consequences"
Petroglyph: "Two by Two"
Portland: "Ride On"
Rain: "Goodnight to the Gillnetters," "Light, Sweet, Crude," "Meet the Neighbors,"
    "Metamorphosis," "Pencil Shavings," "Sacrament (Kitty Brings Supper)" "The Paintball
    War" & "Powdermilk at Thirty-two"
Salal: "Chinook and Chanterelle," "Trapezoids," "Unwanted Creatures" & "The Circle"
Terrain.org: "Evensong," "February Third (Spring Has Many Hungers," & "Still Life"
Windfall: "Stonehenge, WA"

I wish to give large thanks to poet Florence Sage, who reviewed the entire preliminary
manuscript with me, helped me immensely in the big job of making final selections and
changes, and also inspired some of the later poems. Thanks to Florence also for her author's
photo, and to Christine Holbert for her elegant book design. The cover art, from lino cuts by the
late Thea Linnaea Pyle, was first published along with the title poem as a 12" x 15" broadside
by Joe and Marquita Green's wonderful Peasandcues Press in Longview, Washington.

Cover Art: Thea Linnaea Pyle.
Author Photo: Florence Sage.
Book & Cover Design: Christine Holbert.

FIRST EDITION

This and other fine LOST HORSE PRESS titles may be viewed online at www.losthorsepress.org.

LIBRARY OF CONGRESS CATALOGING-IN-PUBLICATION DATA

Names: Pyle, Robert Michael.
Title: Chinook & Chanterelle : poems / Robert Michael Pyle.
Other titles: Chinook and Chanterelle
Description: First edition. | Sandpoint, Idaho : Lost Horse Press, [2016]
Identifiers: LCCN 2016007133 | ISBN 9780996858403 (trade paper : alk. paper)
Classification: LCC PS3616.Y545 A6 2016 | DDC 811/.6—dc23
LC record available at http://lccn.loc.gov/2016007133

Praise lips poetry and love to the very verge.

— *Stefán Hörður Grímsson,* "Day of Reckoning"

To the memory of Thea Linnaea Pyle,
the best chanterelle hunter ever

CONTENTS

CHINOOK & CHANTERELLE

for Thea

What gifts these are
from river and woods. These
coral ones, muscled strumpets, plucked
from the fishers' nets
where the shrunken runs
still shine. And these
golden ones, fluted trumpets, pinched
from the forest floor
where the second-growth hemlocks
still stand. Surely—
we are unworthy of such as these!

But if enjoyment of succulent flesh
is any mitigation, if the tongue's
fierce possession of taste
can be extenuation, if the way
we chew and praise and slurp and swallow
and—say it—worship this fin and stipe,
these silver scales and meaty caps,
can sing the hard shimmer
in the stream can cry the soft glimmer
on the mossy floor can *save* us—
if these gestures make
any difference whatsoever, well,
then maybe we deserve them
after all.

STILL LIFE

On the kitchen windowsill,
bleeding hearts spring
from a vase: the big garden ones
like pink, puffed-up pigtails around
their clitoral white centers; the smaller
wild ones in deeper rose, all pendent
from arcing pedicels.

Different leaves to either side:
fingered fine or coarser, in measure
to their blooms. *Dicentra:* two parts
around that intricate middle. Pollinated
within, they never quite open: just spread,
balloon, reflex, collapse, and drop,
like old hearts everywhere.

Above and behind, two broad green vanes embrace
a flight of "white coral bells, upon a slender stalk"—
lilies of the valley, designed to break
with their unbearable scent
every tame and wild heart, even before
they fall.

POEM

Deprivation is to me as daffodils were to Wordsworth.

—Philip Larkin, interview with the *London Observer,* 1967

That spring we sought the daffodils—
the indigenous little English ones,
restricted now to the Forest of Dean
and a few other spots. The sprouts field
had been plowed before the rain,
and the Bedfordshire clay clung
so thick that we arrived in the wood
several inches taller than we'd begun,
only to find that someone had picked
all the daffodils.

Next spring, big continental daffodils
by the thousands bloomed at Beaulieu,
like solar flares shooting out of Dorset.
Larkin has a point, I guess, that what's left out
can move the heart as much or more
as what's left in. But when it comes
to daffodils and love, I stand with Will:
I'll take surfeit over deprivation
every time.

FEBRUARY THIRD:
SPRING HAS MANY HUNGERS

Foamy banks of snowdrops bloomed,
under siege by honeybees. In the lawn
the purple splay of crocus, on the air
their honey scent.

Careful not to crush the stalks, I crept
across the turf to sniff. Saw a mating
pair of flies on satin petals, then withdrew.
Love deserves its distance, after all.

But the cat, no poet he, rolled among
the nuptial bower, the purple spears
of unborn blooms, the white, the mauve,
and put the coupled flies to flight.

That's when I saw that spring
has more in mind than love: on top,
a shit-fly (as farmers call it);
underneath, a housefly.

Unbonded at their tender tips
(where flies make love and maggots)
they were joined up front instead,
mandible to mortal flesh.

The shit-fly had her by the neck,
sucking his love to a husk. Spring
has many hungers, and the ways
we feed them, in the end, are few.

GIRL, BOOK, BROOK

Outside the pub at Enterprise,
a young girl basks on a rock. Dips
her feet in aspen-dappled brook, sips
her Pepsi, reads her book. Has
a rainbow on her cheek
and a future that will somehow
be touched by this book, this brook.

Downstream a mother walks
her infant son. He pats
the aspen bark and leaf, gets
to know each tree.

A fritillary flits across
the book, buttercups bloom
beside the brook, yellow warbler
"sweet, sweets" above it all. Hoverfly
lights on the back of my hand.

Maybe things
aren't as bad
as I thought.

THE WATERMELON

Too ripe! Leaking in the bottom
of the fridge. Take it out, put it
on a stump. Cleave it four ways
with a very serious knife. Cut
out the center. Eat it in cubes,
four days and nights. Delicious!
Put the rest out in the sun.
Someone will eat it: the calliope
hummingbird, butterflies, beetles.
Or bees. One morning, all gone.

And to think I was just going to toss it.

UPON OBTAINING MY GOLDEN EAGLE PASS

Fifty-one weeks I'd been sixty-two, so why
hadn't I done it yet? Never mind. Carmine,
she of the pretty name and face, was happy
to sell it to me in Asotin. "Senior Pass," it says,
on a picture of cactus flowers, and on the other side,
"Lifetime Pass to all the federal recreational lands"—
the refuges, forests, parks, and all the rest. "Golly!"
I say, and "Hail! Hail to the public lands!"—
those who make us rich beyond measure in rocks
and waters, birds and flowers. Ten bucks for life!
There's never been a better bargain.

PENCIL SHAVINGS

I love the brown butterflies that fly
among canyon walls, where the scent is juniper,
that flit above San Luis Valley's floor
—Nabokov's satyrs, Alamosa wood nymphs—
flecks of fawn and otter on the wing. How
their papery vanes make hope
from nothing more than nectar and dust.

Yesterday I moved my desk, discovered
in a disused drawer a small paper bag:
pencil shavings I'd somehow kept. How
could I throw them in the trash now,
having saved them all this time? The open
window winked. Without a thought, I cast
the cedar chips to the crabshell breeze.

Pale brown butterflies flickered past,
all down to the valley floor of the street—
and for a moment, the scent was juniper.

SHOPPING FOR MEN

"Darn tasty beer," reads the poster for Manny's
Pale Ale, and you know, it is. My friend drives
the truck that delivers the malt to Manny's
Brewery in Georgetown, old Seattle, and that
is good work in the world.

Christmas shopping on foot in Wallingford,
my usual problem: three males left on the list,
and no ideas. "They don't *have* to get *books,*
you know," said my wife. Oh, what to do?

But Tweedy and Popp's Hardware comes
to the rescue. Three tubes of Gorilla Glue,
three rolls of Gorilla Tape. "That takes
care of them," I say, and tick their names
off the list. My labors thus completed,

I walk down to the Blue Star. "Manny's, please,"
I tell the barmaid. "Out shopping?" she asks.
"That's right," I say, "hard work, hard work."
"Well, here's your Manny's, she says, setting
the pint before me, making it all worthwhile.
Darn tasty beer.

LIGHT, SWEET, CRUDE

"The price of light sweet crude is up
ten dollars a barrel," said the radio
this morning. Oil, that is.

"Light sweet crude"—is this the only
entity whose name is made
entirely of adjectives?

"Great Spangled Fritillary" comes
to mind, and "Big Brown Bat"—but
they're tied down by nouns in the end.

Vaguely salacious, "light sweet crude"
might limn relationship these days, how some
folks like to keep romance.

Neither hog bellies nor sugar beets,
grain futures nor carbon credits—
surely no other commodity name

oils imagination, greases desire, lubricates
lust as this one does. For don't we all,
be honest now, like things a little bit
that way?

LLANO DES LOS LOTREROS

I feel changed by the monarchs. Things are different now.

—Thea Linnaea Pyle

Mexican pony munches dry grass on the llano, pink filaree in his hay,
cardinal flowers against the black forest behind. Red warblers shrill
in the tops of the oyamels. Lobo's rope draws tight against his halter.

Three caballeros lie in the yellow grass, laughing softly. Jesus reads
a comic about Las Monarcas, gets the facts from its bad color: come
from El Norte at Dias des Muertes, stay all winter in the firs, then
go back again, time after time, over and over again. They wonder
why turistas come so far to see, pay good wages, just to photograph
what they have known all their lives.

Monarchs pepper the meadow, fill the air itself. You can hear them,
these butterflies—susurrus of thin vanes—and the vegetation rustles
beneath the gentle weight of wings. They fill the firs, so many
to a branch they sometimes break them. One alights on my head.
Someone asks, could a great flight of butterflies sink a ship?
A million couldn't sink a dingy, I say; but the weight of this one
is almost more than I can bear.

Orioles and grosbeaks raid the clumps for their fat. Sediment
of scissored victims mats the forest floor. We bask
against a mossy rock on slope of chips where tree's been cut.
Monarchs bask here too. Unless they gain the warmth to fly
into remaining firs, they'll freeze tonight. Chill is gathering
all about the blessed plain.

If, one fall, the monarchs come and find the firs are gone,
then at least this is true: for a time, this extravagant gesture.

11

STONEHENGE, WA

Sam Hill built this henge of concrete and pebbles
to honor Skamania County's dead from World War I,
just a standing stone's shadow from his lonely mansion,
from the peaches and steeple of his village below. Called
it a monument to peace.

First time I camped here was '81, in a Ryder truck,
twin bed laid crosswise behind the tailgate. Awoke
to basalt breaks on the Oregon side laid out
like breakfast in bed for the eyes.

Next in oh-eight: red and amber truck-lights traced
the Gorge, headlights and horns of freight trains cut
the coffee night, paddle-wheelers and barges plied
the wide dark river. Now, again, a July night in '15.
So what's new?

The sunrise still goes pink, then Mt. Hood, a sundog
over Oregon in between. White-steepled Maryhill still pokes
out of peach trees, white pelicans beyond, in the river.
Biggs still shows neon across the bridge. Columbia still rolls,
and damp yellow grass smells too good to be true.

Stonehenge itself doesn't change. The sarsens still stand
against meadowlark song and wind. All those boys
from Klickitat, one per stone, dead these hundred years,
are still dead.

But here's the deal: so are you. This time,
when I get home, you won't be there.

WHEN THE KILLER HAS NO FACE

I curse your cunning stalker cancer.

—Maxine Kumin, "Elegy Beginning with
Half a Line from Ben Johnson"

When the killer has no face
you've got no one to blame.
And that's just too hard. Better
 to have a brute with a bludgeon,
some psychopath, some would-be lover
crazy with rejection or jealousy. When
the homicide's anonymous
you've got no mugshot for the dartboard
no body to hate, or prosecute.
Easier to have some god
or other to pin it on. Gods, after all,
make the best scapegoats.
Why else bother with such high-
maintenance companions? Oh,
they're useful enough to thank or praise
for, say, this swallow on a post,
this wood nymph winging by. But, really—
where's a god when you need one?

When the killer comes and has no face
you're on your bloody own.

BECOMING THEA

Badly, is how it's going.
When for thirty years
      everything you did
was an act for four hands
and now there are just your two
and the two that are missing
were the ones that knew
what to do and how to do it;
then, all you can do is to try
to be her as well as yourself.

You are probably more clever
than I. You might do it better,
and anyway, I hope you never
have to try.

Ah! Her garden, her kitchen,
her home. Why does it all look
like a burrow in the Tall Grass
Prairie National Park? Oh, I do
hope you never have to try
to become your love who's gone, she
who made sense of the world.
Because if you do, you too
will do it badly.

MAKING A PLACE FOR GRIEF

I'm trying to carve out a place
where this grief can live.
Somewhere between my ribs
or under my diaphragm,
where it can stretch out
and take its time, where
I won't have to see it or talk
with it or visit except on
mutually agreed dates. But
it kicks in bed, and thumps
in my stomach, and pushes
from behind when I stand still.
I'm hoping, these days, that grief
will make a place for me.

PLEASE TOUCH

for Bilak Bokis

Kitty is growing old.
His thick black fur
like the pelt of night,
goes thin and brown,
so when he basks now
he reminds me of the swatch
of beaver fur at the mountain-man show
labeled "Please Touch." And that,
in the sun, is all he asks.

METAMORPHOSIS

Two new kittens saw me off to Texas;
only one ran out when I came home. Bentley
was gone. His brother Bo, ears flat, stared
east, terrified. I took him in. When I went
back out into the night a gray shadow ran
past the porch. Coyotes yipped nearby,
sang beneath the mourning moon
all night long.

Long is the litany of cats that went before:
Milkweed, Brownie, Bridget, Virga,
any number of nameless strays, all run off
to join the coyotes. The highway is hard
on cats and dogs and deer. But coyote
is the great leveler: agent of revenge
for vole and shrew and thrush.

Splitting wood today, I heard an odd sound
from my near woods, like puppies at a den.
Coyote pups, playing in the sun on the bank,
as Bentley had last week; playing, and gnawing,
and growing, as cat transmogrifies
into dog.

THE GIFT

Lawnmower rumbles through June-long grass
pot-gray overcast blocks any sense of summer
black-capped chickadee works unfolding oaks
robin plucks and swallows red huckleberries
cat lies by ivy's curl sated by one large vole
yet watching for another, ever hopeful
that he might once again approach back door
give that guttural purr or sexual snarl
that means "See what a gift I bring for you"
and receive approval that is all his
to ignore.

THAT'S WHAT

So the Swainson's thrushes sing from every compass point,
harmonizing with each other and themselves, two notes in one.

So the baby violet-greens call "Jeepers! Feed me!" from the gourd
above the porch, their parents piping shrill as they comply.

So fledgling hummers ricochet from snowball, oak, and rhodie
whistling "Where next? Where next? Here's where!"

So mock orange drips with too much sweet to swallow,
and honeysuckle soaks what's left in syrup, leaking out
on evening air already thick with fresh cut grass.

Grass, mock orange, and honeysuckle,
thrush and swallow and hummingbird—
So what?

That's what.

THE ROOM OF LOST ITEMS

What if you opened a door
and there was a room
with everything you'd ever lost?
The paper flowers you made
for your mother, that blew
away in the snow.
All the jackets you left on buses.
That scab.
The hats alone would fill a long shelf! The heather
purple deerstalker, the 3X Beaver Stetson smokey,
the Hoss Cartwright 10-gallon that badly needed losing.
Remember that beautiful scarf left in the lecture hall?
The binoculars that were part of your body for 40 years?
The wallets? The gloves? All those things you promised
not to lose.

And then you walk through this door, and they're all here!
Oh, the joy! That special sock! That kitten, those keys . . .
but wait. There are people in here too, and versions
of your heart
in several shapes and states.
And the deal is? You have
to take them all.

TWO BY TWO

On July 7, 2001, at 15:08 Hours Pacific Daylight Time,
I collected a female Lycaena rubidus *and a male* Satyrium fuligonosum,
an intersubfamilial hybrid mating of the Sooty Hairstreak
with Edith's Copper. The pair remained in copulo *as they died.*

—Alvin Ludtke, *News of the Lepidopterists' Society*

When the *nue ardente* consumed Pompeii, they were dozing
   in the afterglow.
When the avalanche took the cabin, they were wrapped up
   in a rug.
When the airplane struck the condo, they were coupled
   in the breakfast nook.
When the rocket hit the hut, they were spooned
   in their marriage bed.

Two of them took their passion for granted when the dam broke,
and two more felt the earth move as the temblor rolled through.
One couple came at the same time the gas line blew.
Another conceived, just before the lights went out.

The forest fire swept the mating swallows in its rush. The bullet
pierced both deer's hearts, at the moment of rut. The dragonfly took
a pair of mayflies on the wing as one, and the toads in amplexus
in the road never felt the tire's tread.

How the honeymoon ended in the isles, when the hurricane arrived.
How the twister brought consummation devoutly to be desired.

It has often been called "the small death," this yielding
to the moment of passion, this giving over everything
to oblivion, this dead loss of the self buried deep in another.

What surprise, then, when sleeping together and the Big Sleep
are the same? Coupled, buckled, merged and melded, wedded,
 welded, linked and twinned, all these ones made two, all perished.

When the camper met the semi, they were bonded
      in the back.
When the elevator fell, they were cleaved
      in the corner.
The thrushes, pressed tail to tail
      when the tomcat pounced.
The she-mouse was not alone
      when the trap snapped shut.

When the net came down, the butterflies were clasped
together at the tip. The pair remained *in copulo* as they died.

TWO ODES FOR AMTRAK

One: Train 14 Is Late

As it often is. But it's not Amtrak's fault, I want to tell
the tired people in the San Jose station. It's the ever-loving
freights they have to wait for; the floods in southern Cal;
the undermined, overused tracks. It's Congress, intent upon
starving its best children, to feed its worst wars.

Tired faces, stuck in laptops and cell phones.
No one seems to notice, painted in roses and hearts,
the great vigas overhead, or J. McQuarrie's late Deco
mural of elegant ladies in an oxcart pulled through
mission mud by Indians and oxen. We embark
just after midnight.

No one in the bar car, the bar being closed.
I watch the end of the movie with my slice
of pizza and an ale I smuggled aboard, as cowboys
and hard drinkers stumble down the stairs, crushed
to see the padlocked bar, then look again
just to be sure. "Bad news," they mutter, on the way
back up to their cars.

Oakland at 1:30, knots of black men outside
the bars, clots of smokers on the platform for a
quick one. At Redding, I get a breath and see
the sun. Mt. Shasta will come by full daylight,
because Train 14 is late. As it often is.
But it's not their fault.

Two: Morning on the Coast Starlight

Sunrise over Lassen's shoulder, snow
stuccoes the Trinity Alps. Blue of the
manzanita, bluer digger pine, rose
pink of California redbud. Green
river canyon past drawn-down reservoirs,
sugar pine ridges, Redding to Dunsmuir.
All this after dewy velvet sheepfolds
and ranks of oaks silhouetted by sunrise
over Lassen's shoulder.

"In twenty years riding this train,"
one woman says, "this is the first time
I've come into Redding in the daylight."
I remember losing this fountain pen
on this train at three A.M., just before
the momentary stop at Redding, the kind
conductor finding it just in the nick of time.

Willows tipped with fresh spring green,
Jeffrey pine sheds rays like old brooms,
Castle Crags shimmer in the sunrise
over Lassen's shoulder. Rare run
indeed, two-thirds around Shasta
in the full light of day.

Trips like this, I wish life
could be a little more like Amtrak: usually
on its rails all right, and often a little slower
than we thought we wanted to go.

UNWANTED CREATURES

Yellowjackets are so numerous this year!
Keeping the doors closed and screens down
will help keep your meeting space
free of these unwanted creatures.

—sign at an eco-resort in Washington's Cascades

Like tigers in the grasses at the Bay of Bengal, having villagers for lunch.
Like bats that flap into bedrooms, leaving rumors of rabies and garlic.
Like wolves who snap up afterbirths, and sometimes even calves.
Like caterpillars of cabbage whites, turning broccoli into lace.
Like bison blamed for bovine TB, and beavers for Giardia.
Like goats in the Galapagos, and elephants in Masai crops.

The flicker hammering the roof at dawn,
 the mockingbird chattering the night away.
The owl who calls *your* name at night, that raven
on the bust of Pallas who makes it all too clear:
Lenore ain't coming back. Like starlings in the city park,
spotted owls in old-growth woods, crows in the cornrows.
Even that nightingale in Berkeley Square must have pissed somebody off.

Like ants in the pantry, bats in the belfry, bees in the bonnet,
bulls in the china shop, fleas on the kitty, ticks on the pooch,
squirrels in the attic, rats in the roof, slugs in the lettuce, crabs
in the crotch, pumas in the playground, coyotes in the lambing
fold, and snakes and spiders pretty much everywhere.

Like prairie dogs digging up the open range, raccoons ransacking
the trash, sea lions with a taste for salmon, rabbits at the carrot patch,
bears at a picnic, chiggers in the grass. 'Possums on the road,
deer through the windshield, skunks on the auto grill. Mosquitoes
at the barbecue, clothes moths in your woolen socks, midges

on a Scottish heath, blackflies blotting out the midnight sun.
Maggots in the Granny Smith, roaches on the kitchen floor, lice
in your daughter's hair. Tapeworms in the gut, virus in the blood.

Like Jews on Kristallnacht, Palestinians on the Temple Mount,
Blacks on the schoolhouse steps, Indians in Dodge,
Tutsis with the Hutu, Muslims with the Serbs,
Catholics in Ulster, gays in Laramie,
women to the Taliban, everyone to someone else—
unwanted, unwanted all.

Be sure and keep the doors closed!

BRETZ'S FLOOD

It starts in the furnace of the core,
rises through the mantle's crush.
Makes the crust, then breaks on through
in plutons, vents, volcanoes. Dike swarms leak
across the land like Vaseline on hot skin.
Congeal in lava flows called Roza,
Elephant Gap and Rattlesnake Ridge,
Umatilla, Pomona, and Selah. Flow,
then freeze in lichen-daubed
entablature and colonnade,
marmot-guarded angle of repose,
all the way to the sea.

After Pangaea, continents surfed
the crusted waves, broke their backs
against far shores, forging the shapes we know.
Plates of the shelf shoulder plates
of the land, bunch them up in the middle,
raise the Rockies from nothing more
than force and dust. Where mountains crumple
upward, before crumbling down again, a moment
comes when, high enough, they tempt
the snows that crown the years. Then press,
and press, and press some more
till glaciers start to move.

As cold goes south, the ice sheets grow,
till half the continent goes under.
Polish, scour, lathe, and grind—leave
sign of ice on granite domes, the scream
of ice on unforgetting stone. Rivers drain
the glaciers, but Clark Fork is plugged:

two thousand feet of ancient ice,
two hundred miles of inland sea.
Then warming, and melting,
time after time for a thousand years,
until some month or minute,
when the dam breaks through!

Then Glacial Lake Missoula is loosed
upon the land. Down pours deluge,
downhill, down-grade, down-map—
ten times the flow of all the rivers of the world.
Cut the coulees, channel scablands,
carve basalt like old black butter; even gouge
that great green slot that we will call the Gorge.

Slash Grand Coulee! Swamp Dry Falls!
Shoot Wallula Gap, whack Beacon Rock,
shatter the very Bridge of the Gods,
before they're even named. Never
so much water, sluicing to the sea,
with such a force of will—sloshing
from wall to black rock wall, from
rimrock to rimrock, four hundred feet deep—
until, the ice all gone,
the river finds its level,
never looking back
at the havoc
it's left behind—

where all
that remains
is geology.

THE BEES IN YOUR WALL

When honeybees find a hole in your living room wall
make a home between rafter and joist between
clapboard and plaster right behind your bookcase
and everyone says honey will leak through
and mice will come and get stuck and stink.
When they tell you to spray or tear out your wall
they have to go or you will surely be sorry except
your scientist friend who says heck just enjoy them.
When your bees persist through winter after winter
survive all the talk about mites and fungus and colony
collapse wiping out honeybees everywhere else.
When you move your oil tank and find the wall behind
is rotten from the rain and a carpenter comes who is also
a lover of bees and he rebuilds the wall *around* the hive
and makes for them little yellow porches, and like good bees
they seldom come into your house and hardly ever sting.
When the bees in your wall disperse on the air
to pollinate your pears your currants your blueberries
then swarm and your beekeeper friend catches
the swarms and he gives you honey in return.
When the bees in your wall give you company
and songs in summer both soft and shrill
and a sense of things that go on and on
then you know your friend was right
and you tell all the others
it's none of their beeswax.

KENAI

Life comes soft here; life comes sharp.

The moss on the boughs and the floor and the logs
grows as soft as the down on your leg,
and the purr of the stream, the spit-whistle song
of the thrush, what the chickadee said,
fall as soft on my ear as a kiss or a whisper
inviting my body to bed.

But the clubmoss and sprucelings erupt from the duff
with the sharpness of millions of pins,
and the devil's club thicket surrounding
this alder is sharp as original sin,
and the four-hundred notes of the winter wren's song
pierce the air like a tooth breaking skin.

Life comes sharp here; life comes soft.

But the mosquito's suck and the bracken fern's rust
and the broken heart's sink and the sunken boat's moan
and the composting world of the lost and the found
make the softness and sharpness the same,
and the foliose lichen and each crustose soul
run together in rot's holy name.

PLEDGE DRIVE

I know they are necessary,
as mosquitoes and viruses are necessary.
I know this philistine country
would never support the public airways,
would leave them out in the cold to flounder
and die, would no more tolerate
a radio license (as Britons do)
than pay a tax on air itself.
I know all this. And yet,
few words strike deeper dread,
few phrases make me tremble more,
than these:
"It's Pledge Drive!"

I listen.
I cringe.
I pledge.

"PEDESTRAINS ON ROADWAY"

sign on Savage Road, Cascade Head

First there were those pesky bicycles.
What a menace! You couldn't hear them,
and all of sudden, they'd be on top of you.
Then came roller skates, and skateboards,
and worse, rollerblades: pure, silent murder
on wheels. Oh, I've adapted. I watch myself,
look left and right, ahead, behind.
But I'm afraid it's all over now.
There's just no defense against
these pesky *pedestrains:* try as I might
to keep out of their way, I know I'm a goner.
They're what's going to get me
in the end.

IN OREGON

High in the pitchy spruces
outside my cabin
two creatures call:
"Chickadee!"
"Chickaree!"
That's all.

DANKE SCHOEN

We walk the shore of Brainard Lake, then into the edge
of the wild. Mom's after mushrooms, I'm hunting
butterflies, Bud bounces back and forth between us.
Mother finds the biggest king boletus she's ever seen:
five pounds, and not a worm. Gives it to me to carry.
Charging up ahead, as a young lad will, I meet
a German couple coming down. *"Ach du lieber!"*
says the man, *"So schoen ein Steinpilz!"* He holds
out his hands. I hand it over for a look.
"Danke schoen!" he gasps, wide-eyed, and turns
downhill. I stand open mouthed, speechless.

"Was that my mushroom?" Mom almost wails
when she catches up, knowing it was. Hasn't forgiven
me yet, and Mom's been gone these fifty years.

RIDE ON
(LEAVE THE DRIVING TO US)

Ride on, Big Gray Dog, ride on.
Ride on, you long metal box on wheels, ride on, ride on.

Ride on, people of the alleys, streets, and farm towns, you mothers with small children eating Baby Ruths for dinner, ride on. Ride on old man with useless legs, losing your pants as you slide down the steps for a smoke when the rest get out for theirs, ride on. Ride on you scarred black man, blonde woman, so loud, your profane repartee so loud in the back of the big gray dog where you've found a refuge and an entourage, your laughs so loud and cackling in the dark, ride on. Young roofer who asks me for pen and paper and draws tattoos, almost speechless, hungry, downing chips and Coke on my two bucks, ride on. Ride handsome boy with a journal, never out of Oregon, to your fiancée in Florida. Ride, old hippie with a club foot and braces; ride, you goateed philosopher dumpster diver with heroic B.O., reading Umberto Eco and telling your grinning seatmate about the Old and the New Testaments and how Jesus loved Mary Magdalene, him telling you about CIA sex slaves, ride on.

Ride, Dog, ride.

Ride to the sordid lean-tos, squalid stations, the Denny's, the McDonald's, the Baker City Truck Corral where the drivers always have the same tables and waitresses. Ride through heavy rain and moonrise, heat and sunset, past fawn pronghorns and white pelicans. Ride you old woman with two coats who wants to buy lipstick and gets up for your stop hours early every time, blocking the aisle; ride you young woman with heartburn who gives the old one your lipstick and cradles your silent hungry child.

Ride on you consternated, patient drivers with your service pins and gray pressed suits and weary patter, remembering the strike and the snipers and dying to retire, who change in Denver, Salt Lake, Boise, Portland, ride on, ride on, ride on, ride on.

Ride, night-dog. Ride, day-dog.

You man with the small girl who slept bare-footed and pillowless on the bare dirty floor in the chaos of the Denver depot, who holds her now in the back among the loud coarse happy riders, ride on. You young pretty mother with two little boys and dirty pillows going all the way to Michigan, ride, and you bawling babies heading three nights to some other place, ride on. On and on.

Ride on you teenage girl in long black velvet gown with tattered hem and no shoes, met by two police cars in Ogden, smiling and waving back at your new friends. You people who joke about the drugs you've known and don't have, who rush out at every stop into spontaneous combustion of the drug you do, ride on.

Ride, roofer, ride. Ride, writer. You weepers, laughers, coughers. Ride, all you who ride and ride and ride the Big Gray Dog.

Ride on, little Latina, your mother across the aisle, your brother behind, your sweet brown head pressed into my side, ride on.

MEET THE NEIGHBORS

You ask about my neighbors?

Well, let's see. On Maple Street, there are the *Acers: macrophyllum, circinatum,* and *pseudoplatanus.* And over on Oak? *Quercus robur, rubra, bicolor,* and *garryanna. Alnus rubra* and *Betula pendula* live at the corner of Birch and Poplar, kitty-corner from *Populus trichocarpa.* Up above loom the conifer clan: *Tsuga heterophylla, Pseudotsuga menziesii, Chamaecyparus lawsoniana,* and Sitka spruce; down below dwell *Dicentra formosa, Hedera helix,* and *Vancouveria hexandra;* youth-on-age, fairy bells, fringecup, meadowsweet, and sweet woodruff. 'Tween tree and herb, those nice Bushes: *Corylus cornuta, Symphoricarpos albus, Oemleria cerasiformis,* and the whole *Rubus* clan: *parviflorus, spectabile, armeniacus,* and *ursinus.* And here come

the herps: top of the morning, *Taricha!* Afternoon, *Ensatina!* Good evening, chorus frogs! And the butterflies: wave to *Limenitis lorquini.* Tip your hat to *Celastrina echo.* And there go those swallowtail boys, *rutulus, eurymedon,* and *zelicaon,* not to mention their cousin, Clodius the Parnassian, hanging out by the bleeding hearts. We could go on forever—there are lots of folks around here. But mustn't neglect the Douglases, fir and squirrel; the Townsends, vole, mole, and chipmunk; Mrs. Swainson the Thrush, Mr. Wilson the Warbler, and that vireo pair, the Huttons. *Buteo, Bubo, Corvus,* and *Turdus; Oncorhyncus* and *Phalacrocorax,* down by the bridge.

Let's see—who else? *Canis latrans, Lynx rufus, Procyon lotor,* all going out on the night shift; and, of course, that whole *canadensis* bunch: *Lutra* the otter, *Castor* the beaver, *Cervus* the Elk, and bunchberry *Cornus.*

Plus a shout-out to the little folks, salt of the earth: *Arion ater, Limax maximus, Ariolimax columbiana, Vespericola columbianus, Monodenia fidelis, Prophysaon foliolatum, Haplotrema vancouverense—*

all the lovely snails and slugs of the neighborhood damps.

Oh, I have many neighbors, all right.
Even some people, I'm told—
though I seldom see them, myself.

SACRAMENT (KITTY BRINGS SUPPER)

Band-tailed pigeons darken the sky
this year, as they used to say
about passenger pigeons. Flood
through, oak to tall oak, stuffing
acorns like popcorn. Then, disturbed
by the slamming screen door, erupt
again, snowing small white feathers.

Kitty mostly devils voles, leaves
the birds alone, but has caught
pigeons before. This one he brings
inside, decorates the dining room
like aftermath of a pillow fight.

After all that, eats just a bite, leaves
the rest for me. A little more plucking,
a bottle of Pinot Gris, a hot skillet: liver,
heart, the gizzard with its acorns;
big purple breast, plump little drumsticks,
all with leeks and butter. Mmm, what a bird,
the band-tail. *What a cat.*

P.S. Today, he catches a mole, half his size,
and brings it to me. Thanks, Kitty: I'm good.

EVENSONG

There are times I do love this city.
Coming out of the holiday book fair into the Park Blocks,
milling with the other authors in the vague rain.
And this great racket of crows! Caws,
rattles, churrs, and shrieks, all tumble
out of the black mass overhead.
Hundreds of crows,
gathering, circling, settling
into the tops of the plane trees, gossiping
with one another, catching up. Calling out
to the evening, to the damp sky,
so loud, so present, everyone is looking up:
the homeless, the hipsters,
and all these authors, their voices stilled.
One low sycamore leaf twirls on its stem
in the darkening breeze.

NEWS PHOTO OF SOMEONE I DIDN'T KNOW

The headline: "Pickup stolen in Mississippi, recovered
in Long Beach." Damian Mullinix caught the shot, two
policemen looking down, pursed lips, creased brows,
a third bending into the cruiser. And there between them,
framed in the V between the open door and the chassis,
the woman: handcuffed, dark hair tossed across
her pretty face beneath the flashing cherry top.

It's that face that haunts me. Just 32, neck taut, cheeks creased,
and her mouth—open, downturned, as if about to wail,
or in the certain knowledge that a train or a bear or a brute
is fast upon her. And her eyes: only "haunted" says it—cast
back, ever looking over her shoulder. How did I get here?
they say. What now?

But her trainwreck has already happened; this is just
the aftermath. The truck is stolen, she's just used meth,
she's a convicted sex offender who failed to register
with the police.

Jessica Hagerty, how did you come to this?
Where are you now? Have you ever been sadder
than you are in this picture that I cannot forget?
Have you ever been happier?

MISSIONARY

One hundred thirty-six kinds of birds.
That's what the natives knew
from their sounds alone. And every plant
had a name, and a use.

"Nothing but what's out there in the forest!"
is what the missionary said the natives had.
He hacked his way in, to change all that.

If there were such a thing as hell
someone in this picture would be on the way—
and it wouldn't be the Indians.

SUPPLIES

Speeding up the 12, past daffodil fields at Mossy Rock,
I make the Cispus Center just ten minutes late for dinner.
But what's this? Why is everyone here in uniform or caps?
Forest Service, BLM—where are all the sixth graders,
chowing down on turkey, spuds, and apple sauce, awaiting
my annual Bigfoot talk with bated breath or sullen curiosity?
Ah . . . I see. I've driven this hundred miles one week early.
Bummer!
Or is it? There's the whole Gifford Pinchot National Forest
up there tonight, and I have supplies: sleeping bag, beer, binoculars—
and a banana!

UNINTENDED CONSEQUENCES

To make the channel deep for ships the Army Corps pumped out the sand from riverbed and stacked it up in spoil islands in midstream. And to the new hotels of sand came cormorants and terns to nest and then they fed their chicks on salmon smolts.

To save the lions of the sea the NOAA said they can't be shot and so their numbers grew and grew and all the docks are swaddled with their blubbered bulks, the airways clogged with barks and roars, and lions eat their fill of salmon up the Gorge.

So now the Army Corps is shooting birds and oiling nests and bogus Orca bellies up instead of scaring lions off and one sea lion basks upon its floating wreck, as others of its kind get shot beneath the dam. Everything we touch comes back to haunt the best laid plans, as every tim'rous beast comes home to eat the hand that shoots it. People of the river towns look on and shake their heads and mutter how in hell did those guys get it wrong again, and turn away, and hawk, and spit.

And so I think of every double-crested cormorant that came and bred because we made the habitat, of every lion of the sea that fouls a dock or eats a fish because we gave it what it needs, and how we're going to take it back and give them both hot lead instead, and *claim* the fish and *take* the dock and *make* the fix, and then, and then, and then, guess what? We'll start the whole damn thing again.

To make the channel deep for ships . . .

OUT OF ITS ELEMENT

We might say that about the rustic bunting,
fifth time in Washington, alone
among the juncoes at our feeder, far,
far away from Siberia.

Or the vermilion flycatcher caught out
in the frosts of Redmond, a thousand
miles north of the acacias and saquaros
it knows.

Take that red-throated loon, grounded
in the road, wet asphalt taken for water,
lift-off impossible. Almost put my eye out
on the way to the river.

Wouldn't you say that an ostrich, marooned
in a sodden northern pasture with a herd
of alpacas and llamas, was way out
of its element?

We can get that way too, you know.
Far from home, adrift, alone. Away,
away from all that matters.

GULLS AT LUNCH

Again and again that ring-billed gull drops
a mussel to the beach from on high. It's got
the idea, but doesn't understand about "hard."
As it veers over the condos with their concrete
decks, I cry, "Yes! There! Drop it there!" But no,
it's back to the sand, where the bivalve just bounces.
Yet, lo! Finally the big mussel pops open.
"So there," says the gull, as it cleans up every bit.

Meanwhile, down the beach, a western gull stands
gullet-stuffed with an old rotting starfish. Two legs
hang out. Its gape at extremity, the bird can't get
the sea-star up *or* down. It makes my jaws ache,
just to watch. At last he spits out his meal
onto the sand. And with raucous bonding cries,
the gull and his mate dismember
what could not be swallowed whole.

At the parking lot the moocher gulls hover,
cry, and light on people's cars. A herring gull
dragging one wing catches my pity. I toss
it the fat from a chunk of ham, and all the gulls flap
onto my hood—including the gimp, who can fly
just fine. But not to worry; that fat I rejected got
one more gull through the night.

We sometimes forget how it's all about getting,
all of the time, for most. Unlike some, who have time
to write poems about such things.

WHAT THE SUN DID

High above Mud Bay
on the Third of March
crept over the ground
and turned the moss
chartreuse.

AGAIN THE SUN,

the September sun. A skipper levitates
past the bedroom window to the right,
thistledown floaters fall over the field.
Shadows of vultures blot the abandoned
lawn. Black walnut leaves, breeze-tossed
yellow confetti. Skipper to the left. Eight
mergansers cut the blue sky into quilt blocks.

The September sun is hot on my knees. All
these things, all day long, day after day.
And still you're gone.

DISAPPOINTMENTS IN THE POTATO LINE

I

Always at Christmas there was *rotmos*
at my friend's Yuletime party. Nothing else,
not the potato sausage from Ballard,
the *sylte* or *skottbullar* or *rullepolse,*
all these meats slathered in lingonberries;
not the pickled herring or the English cheeses;
not the *krumkaka,* the almond ears, the *pepparkokar;*
not even the lemon curd *sandbackels,* nor yet
his famous custard that he refuses
to refrigerate all night long, then serves at breakfast,
Salmonella be damned. None of the provender
prepared by that plate-licking Swede
in his annual orgy of holiday fare provokes
quite the rapture, the ooh's and aah's, the drool
daubed just in time or caught with a *krumkaka,*
as the *rotmos.* This unprepossessing mash,
this off-white, oleo-yellow mush of rutabagas and potatoes
goes down so easy with sweets and fats,
stanches the sugar, soaks up the grease,
makes a landing pad in the pylorus
for one more pickled herring. This year
eveything was in place until I reached
the end of the line: what's this? No *rotmos!*
An absence of rutabaga, an impoverishment
of potatoes. Just then I felt
something go out of Christmas,
as I had, say, in 1956, when
my mother and Santa Claus both left.
With luck, the *rotmos* might be back next year.
But Christmas as it was before,
never.

II

It wasn't always about the donuts,
as some people think. Nor was it a matter
of mere sentiment. How to explain
the Spudnut Man? There he was,
perched on a Cushman tri-scooter
with a cab and a box on the back,
like the one the Popsicle Man drove.
Through the dusk of our asphalt blocks
came the Spudnut Man, his bell tinkling,
making mouths water Pavlov-style
before dispensing donuts at our doors.
Who among us could resist
his big, glazed, potato donuts?

Later I worked at a donut shop. The difference
was like Red Delicious to Cox's Pippin: flaccid,
cloying blimps of fat, the glazed I sold
couldn't touch the plump and luscious wares
of the Spudnut Man.

In later years, northing or southing
the Oregon coast, we always stopped
at a little nook in Lincoln City's strip
where we knew
that the very best donuts might be had
from an old German couple who made them:
"Potato donuts," read the faded sign.
But last time the sign said "Closed." And now
there are no signs at all. Long lost, that nook,
that tinkling bell. Long lost.

III

It should have been delicious.
The words sounded so good
together, like strawberries and cream,
dark chocolate and coffee. How
could it not be sublime?
Peach potato pie: a dish
of perfect cadence, ingredients aligned
in alliterative harmony. Doesn't
it make you smack your lips, how
those succulent syllables roll out?
Peach potato pie.

Writers ought to know a good dish
when they hear it. So why
didn't they like it? Polite,
was the way they picked
the peaches from the pie. "Nice crust,"
said one. "Interesting texture," another.
But on the whole my pie fell flat. It was love
that brought us together— love
of one another, of good words, good food.
But love was not enough to rescue
my peach potato pie.

Their common stodgy pallor aside,
peaches do not marry with potatoes
as rutabagas do, and a fluffy crust
does not a Spudnut make. Next time
I'll leave the peaches to the cobbler, the spuds
to the rotmos. Such a mush! Like marriage,
when minds that seem akin collide
instead of blending. Beware
the dish whose very name is lyric.

IN SEQUOIA, IN 1969

I became a ranger where the Big Trees grow.
Took visitors to Tokopah Falls, through Crystal Cave,
around Crescent Meadow (John Muir's favorite) at dawn.
Days off, it was *UP* into wilderness: High Sierra Trail,
Heather Lake, even Mineral King, before Disney tried
to wreck it. Then back to the Sherman Tree, to answer
the same old questions: *How old is it? How big is it? What
are all the black marks on the bark? Where are the bathrooms?*

Led a hundred people an hour around the Congress Trail.
Took ninety, one time, *inside* a hollow giant, all burned out,
but alive. And in the circular grove where John Muir led
John Burroughs to hear the hermit thrush—"a religious beatitude,"
said John o'Birds to John o'Mountains—the hermit piped
for us too, every time, as soon as we all shut up.

APHIDS

Gray aphids, lined up three deep along the stem,
suck nasturtium's sap and give back honeydew
for their sweet-toothed shepherds, the ants. I nip
the tip of nasturtium's spur, steal a drop of syrup
from the nectary's deep hold. Such sweet and spicy
stuffs these orange and yellow blooms give up.

But I'll never know the real thing, how
the honeydew tastes refined, until
like the greedy ants I suck it
from the sucking bugs
themselves.

FIREFLY

I saw the green light go on in my hands. Scuttling
in the undergrowth, with its lamp left on, it was easy
to follow. Plucked up, it poured bioluminescent
paint all over my palm. Then flew, flashing, up,
toward Cassiopeia. But before all that, I held
the firefly, and the green light came back into the world.
Closing my eyes, I saw it again, against the lids,
against the dark.

NO REGRETS

shouts the star from the cover of the magazine.
How lovely to have no regrets at all.

No little brother you treated badly, or sister you embarrassed
just for fun. No telephone call you made with friends
to the last girl in the world to deserve your taunts.
No kid you roughed up for his long hair, when five years later
yours would be twice as long.

How sweet for you to have no man or woman
you ever misused for sex or weakness or dullness,
no tedious friend you ditched on a long road trip,
no animal that got less than it needed
because of your lazy ways.

How nice for you not to miss your last chance
for a moment alone with your mother, dragged off
for a haircut before she was dragged off
to the hospital, when you could have said "No!"

To have never said "no" to a lover, or "yes,"
when the other word would have been the right
one. Never rued the ill word spoken, the kind
one left unsaid.

How dare you say "I have no regrets?"
How would you ever dare
to say you do?

WORLD TURNS TO STRAW

And so this long autumn goes on,
turning the world to straw. In the meadow
under the Goat Wall old barley bends
and clatters against knapweed in the breeze.
Ringed by dark pines, broken with aspens
and yellow-green cottonwoods, the meadow rolls,
this sea of straw. Yes,

it was barley took the place of mountain
flowers and sedges; an old plough rusts at the edge.
Closing branches creak and whine, nuthatches toot
the minutes gone, old field settles into permanent crop
of knapweed. In all this sere sea, just two patches of color:
orange stake, pink ribbon: field marks
for what comes next.

CITY OF ROCKS

California Trail, Idaho, 1850

A valley like the crowded mouths
of oreodonts, before dentition settled down.
Between the wagons and the safety of the Humboldt,
miles and miles away, stood these jumbled jaws,
where none but a crazy scout could imagine
passage for the wheels. Families stopped, huddled
in the shade, scratched charcoal hope on walls
of rock. This maw was hard on hope, sucked it up
like marrow from a desert bone. Those teeth!
Gleaming like filed ivory against the night.
There are no lullabies in granite.

Sleep came hard in the City of Rocks,
that maxillary trainwreck. What gnashing
in the night there? What cringing
from the dawn's cruel truth?

It might be so, that no one will know that terror again,
traversing row on row of jutting rocks toward God
knows what. It might be so, that everyone needs to know.

ACCIDENT ON NEAHKANIE

I heard the sirens, far off, as I began the climb
up Neahkanie Mountain. Soon it was upon me:
sheriff's jeep, then ambulance, and another.
The cars pulled over to let them by. Traffic gelled
ahead, all the way up. Lights flashed

in the gathering dusk, yellow, red, blue.
A fire engine came, two, three, and a cruiser.
Pickups of volunteers, EMTs with axes and satchels.
Boys ran up the road to see what they could see,
and never would forget.

A Belgian went up the line to check it out.
"They collided like this," he said, hitting
his fists together. "And his heart . . . they're making
him alive again. It might be long time,"
was how he said it.

I pulled out of that clot, turned around, took
old 101 instead. On my way over Three Rocks Road
toward the coast, the thinnest crescent moon I'd ever seen
made its sad way down.

PLATYPUS BECOMES ONE WITH WATER

The otters' ability to disappear, to melt into the water,
to slip into the background as if they had never been there . . .

—Adam Nicolson, *National Geographic*

And not only otters!
It might have been my graceless slip
that made it dive, and then stay down.
My brutish lurch to riverbank, when
someone called "Come see!"

I'd lurked by a bridge, the best spot,
I'd heard, while others, upstream, watched
its duckbill, webfoot, beavertail,
to heart's content. All I saw was
silky pellet melting into murk,
as platypus and water merged.

Ten seconds sooner, I'd have seen
that crazy mammal well ("some
Tasman trick," they'd called it in London).
But look at it this way: one second later,
and I'd have missed it
altogether.

POLLEN NATION

Night-blooming cereus opens white flower to tippling bat
like petticoats parted for a ravenous lover.
Fringed prairie orchid takes the tongue of hawkmoth,
gives back nectar, so that inconstant, impassioned hawk
carries fringed prairie sperms to the next tasseled bloom.
Bog orchids entrust their pollen to mosquitoes—
that's one reason, at least, for their existence.
White-winged doves drink the nectar of saquaros,
ensuring purple fruits to come. Hummingbirds,
of course, pollinate a thousand plants—*Aquilegia,
Delphinium, Fuchsia*, and *Ribes* for starters. But
it's the bees who move the bulk of those golden grains,
bees and wasps and flies and bee-flies and hoverflies
and butterflies, and the many moths who service
the night-bloom.

Pollination: how flowers fuck,
through their happy go-betweens, the insects,
birds, and bats. How plants make it
through the night.

HEAVY METAL BAND

When I took my wedding ring off at last
my friend said "you're removing
heavy metal from your hand,"
and he was right. Never has a finger felt
so stripped, as if it were my hand,
not my heart, that was bereft.
But when it was gone—
that pale and dented finger stripped
of its heavy metal band—
it was my heart that came free.

DUFFY'S DECK

17 August 2014

Only crows to be heard. Merganser
duckling, long bill ring-tipped,
pale neck and belly down, strange
to be all by itself, out there
in the milky way of knotweed petals,
nebulae of cottonwood leaves,
riding the uptide flow.

27 July 2015

Yellow-striped jumping spider leaps to my knee.
Steller's jay vaults the river, which loops
around the gravel bar under alders and elms,
ninebark and knotweed, then slingshots
down to the bay, on this 90-degree afternoon.
Wait till winter! When the river roars through here,
almost up to the deck, and I take my pint inside,
into dim orange light and endless Irish tapes.

But for now,
out here on Duffy's deck, with the crows,
the mergs, the jays, as the day drops
through 80, to 70, and more,
perfection seems possible.

Yet still my pint runs out.

AT THE DUCK

The nocturnal people of Skamokawa,
they're good eaters, occupy their chairs and bar stools
with authority. They drink, they laugh, they go
outside to smoke. Their dreams may be long gone,
but they dance for all that, drink beneath the plastic
Christmas lights, and their karaoke is much better
than you ever thought it would be.

TV in every corner plays Animal Planet, Fox News,
sports, and weather. The waitress sets up pool balls
as a Jimmy Buffett with a belly and a voice sings out
from four lonely days in a brown L.A. haze, and the DJ,
who sings every other song, is the Walrus. Such
is night life on the other side of K-M Mountain,
and the halibut isn't bad.

THE SHRIVING OF THE SWALLOWS

At this old cattle ranch
meadowlark pipes in bunchgrass
wind comes up with clouds, takes
the air below a hundred
with seventeen drops of rain. Barn
swallows nest beneath the eaves,
tree swallows in a box, cliffs in the gables.
New fledglings tumble out each day.
Swallows cut the restless air
between schoolhouse and bunk,
weave among the old white boards,
screaming, chittering, singing their glee
to be out of those louse-ridden nests,
their joy at the cooling of the day.
Strung up in the frantic criss-cross
of the swallows, uncertain of my crime,
I am shriven.

THE SOUNDS OF SANTA CRUZ DE LA SOLEDAD

Dogs. One barks, they all bark.
The neighbor's radio, incessantly on,
to scare the squirrel; sometimes rock,
sometimes medieval chant, whatever comes.
Roosters: one crows, they all crow.
Canyon wren's cascading trill, social flycatchers
socializing. Donkeys. One brays, they all bray.
The town crier on the PA in the plaza.
A *banda* band in the bandstand on Sunday.
More dogs. Hooves, shod, on cobblestones.
Children. One laughs, they all laugh. Old
pickups and cars slowing for the pebble speed bumps.
"Zeta! Zeta! Zeta Gaz!" again and again on
the propane truck's speakers. Gilded
woodpecker, blue mockingbird, grackles,
English sparrows in the eaves. One peeps,
they all peep. More dogs.

GOING AERIAL IN AJIJIC

Morning, sip coffee on the new terraza, watch
Cristina chase butterflies around the yard. Cages
them until she has enough, then fetches
the guide to give them names—Little Yellow,
Ardent Crescent, Large Orange—then lets them
go free, and they all fly away.

Afternoon, sip Modelo in concrete stands,
watch David chase flies across the field. Bags
one, retires the other side. At bat,
he gets a single, then a run. One ball fouls
into the bull ring, another homers into the market.
Most baseballs slap a fielder's mitt. But some,
like butterflies, go free, and fly away.

THE PAINTBALL WAR

All in the valley of Death
Rode the six hundred.

—Alfred Lord Tennyson, "The Charge of the Light Brigade"

Into the City Watershed
rode the eighty, National Guard and local lads
and dads. Theirs not to reason why,
theirs but to have a good time.

In full battle regalia rode the eighty,
camo and goggles and hunting gear,
armed with the mighty paintball
guns, each the other to smite
and smear, to simulate gore, to show
who killed the other.

Into the forest rode the eighty, and a good time
was had by all. Two hours, two skirmishes,
twenty thousand rounds of paint, onto each other
and into the groundwater. "It was just like
a real battle," said the warriors, except
that all the eighty rode back.

Onto the scene dropped the engines of war—
two big Blackhawks. All looked up in awe
when the helicopters landed.
"A great experience for the local kids,"
said the paper. And this came to pass
at Christmastime, as troops and weapons
were building up. Into the Gulf

went a boy I know, who used to hunt
butterflies with me. Gone to guard
prisoners of the coming war. "We wish,"
said his parents' Christmas card,
"he'd never traded his butterfly net
for a machine gun."

WHO?

As leaders of nations meet to parley the state of the Earth
and my country sends a general, keeping him out of the way back home
since he might oppose the latest war;

As penguins show up in Alaska, and the Antarctic umbrella frays,
and air and water run together in a gelid blend, half the forests burn
and the other half are cut to keep from burning;

yet, as soft petals still unfurl, and bright wings dance on mountain air,
brooks and breezes bring cool scent of balsam and hay, and keys of ash
and samaras of maple, acorns and hickories and hazelnuts yet fall
on forest floors *in spite of everything,*

I ponder these verbs from the *Earth Charter:*

*care affirm accept ensure promote secure protect adopt
safeguard control prevent take action avoid advance convert
reduce reuse recycle rely relieve require resolve restore respect
support empower enable strengthen uphold fulfill create enhance
integrate eliminate implement demilitarize serve act honor . . .*

and I ask,

who will?

TRAPEZOIDS

I'm on psychopharmaceuticals and in the country.

—Harvey Shapiro, "The Ticket"

"Bright flickering things danced inches from my face,"
said my friend. "They looked like trapezoids."
I suggested ghost moths, known to spiral close and shimmer.
"No, they were geometric," he said. "And right there!"

I saw my friend again the other day. He'd been up
to the secret place by the falls. "And guess what?
They were there again!" His wife saw them too,
but not so clearly. "My medicine made them blurry," she said.
What medicine was that, I asked? "Ecstasy," she said.

Had my friend taken that, when he saw the trapezoids?
"Yes," he said. "But that had nothing to do with it."
He wants me to come along next time. "I'll show
you the spot, and we'll see if the trapezoids are there."
Without the ecstasy, I wondered? "Right," he said.
"Maybe next time we'll just take mushrooms."

POEM FOR PUMAS

a mighty will stands paralyzed

—Rainier Maria Rilke, "The Panther"

Mountain lions, carved in stone, prowl the mountain West.
Hewn by romantics, cat-lovers, hunters, and those
who never have seen one at all, they bide their time,
standing in for all the hurts great cats have known.

In Sinclair, Wyoming, four sandstone panthers hold up
a fountain stem, spew water into the bowl below.
In Colorado Springs, a pack of pumas guards a flagpole,
never batting an eyelash, or the banner overhead.

In Bellingham, one fat catamount howls on the lap
of a fat, howling man. They howl for all the lions gone,
howl for the bounties that he was paid, howl for the hell of it.
Hearing the howls in their bones of stone, all the pumas stretch—
and spring.

GOODNIGHT TO THE GILLNETTERS

And so we go drifting at fishdark. Remember us.

—Irene Martin, *Legacy and Testament*

And so it comes to this.
A hundred years and half again
these small sleek craft have plied
the river's swells and rolls, cast
their nets at fishdark, to drift
the drifts their fathers knew
and theirs before, as moon or sun
or mostly rainy gray rode shotgun.
Crossed the current, doubled back
then reeled the nets and pulled the catch
if any catch there was to pull.
And then went home and dried the nets
and fixed the nets and tickled the engine
and paid some bills or put them off
and then put in and did it all again,
as tides and openings allowed.

This county's forests gone to pulp,
the dairies nearly gone as well,
and yet the fishers persevere. Their low-sterned
wooden boats still growl their way from slip
to drift to tide, to runways known by heart
by man and boat from all these years
of making life in town and home by taking
precious life in turn. All life means taking
life to live, and this hard-working life still
works. These fishing-family lives still work.

Or did, but now it comes to this: the thud
of gasoline motor stilled, the whap of wave
on bow and stern, but echoes off a faded
chart. Wake gone slack, the cork and lead lines
all reeled in, their drums at rest, these boats bob
lonely on their last ebb tide, as darkness swamps
the river night, and all the navigation lights
just flicker out.

People!
This isn't Wynken, Blynken, and fuckin' Nod
we're talking about, who sailed off
in a wooden shoe one night to fish for
the herring fish on a river of crystal light!
These are real people with real names,
and nets of twine and nylon, not silver
and gold. Names like Haven, Stephan,
Goodell, and Crouse; Tarabochia, Clark,
and Souvenir; like Emery and Bond,
Martin and Holland, Bergseng, Backman,
Budnick, and Blix; like Stanley, McKinley,
Kuller, and Quigley, Pedersen, Olsen,
and Ostling. And these are just the ones
still here, still willing to fish
from Wahkiakum's docks.

At least thirty families, in just one county
of four thousand souls! How many more,
up and down the whole river? One gillnetter,
sick at heart, calls it rural genocide, when
all the salmon go for sport instead of family jobs.
This was one place eating close to home

made sense, supporting local people.
And the fish, dams willing, came back.

Listen! you governors of men, commissioners
of fish, you wreckers of the good and ancient ways:
How dare you steal this commonwealth
of water, land, and man, this comity of people,
fish, and river? How dare you?

And this I'd like to know as well: how
will you show your face downstream,
when the faces of the fisherfolk
turn away?

On January 12, 2013 the Washington Fish and Wildlife Commission voted 7-0 to phase out gillnetting on the main-stem Columbia River. The Oregon Fish and Wildlife Commission soon followed suit, and both governors agreed.

IMAGINATION

How can I tell if I'm in love?
asked the man of his cat.
Oh, that one's easy, the cat said.
It's when your imagination makes
an ant into a rhinoceros, a grassblade
into a Douglas-fir, and the absence
of her email into a Russian novel.
It'll turn a beetle into a bulldog,
the cat went on, a clamshell into a bombshell,
and a good woman into anything
you can possibly imagine. I guess
I'm in love then, said the man
to his brontosaurus.

GIRL WITH GOAT CHEESE IN HER HAIR

It could be that it got there when she was bringing
the goats home to milk one night and a truck zoomed
by and spooked the goats who ran into the river
where they bounced over the rocks till their milk set up
and the girl pulled them out and led them home to bed,
but on the way in the dark she tripped on a root
and bumped her head on one nan's rump and that one butted
the next one's bag and so on down the line
which made them all loose their curdled milk
on leaf and tree and log and stone
and girl.

Or it could be she was breaking bread with a boy
when he said for the first time "I love you,"
and, well, that was how.

WASHING THE WEDDING DISHES

The first time I married we got Rosenthal. Just eighteen,
we somehow selected well at the Denver Dry—that smoky-
rimmed pattern called "Evensong," symbolic platinum ring
around the rim. Bone china, settings for fourteen
with all the bits, pepper-and-salt to turkey platter.
After the wedding, they went into a safe, where they stayed
until long after the divorce.

The second time I married it was Portmerion, heavy ceramic
from the English potteries—the antique flowers and butterflies
of "Botanic Garden," bought in Bath by her grandmother,
service for eight. There were eight at table that New Year's Eve.
As I washed up after midnight, the whole stack *hydroplaned*
off the breadboard and onto the kitchen floor, in one almighty
New Year's crash. Even the turkey platter with the swallowtail.

The third time I married, no one gave us dinnerware. She had
her blue-bordered International "Celebration Service" for twelve,
and her own wedding china for special: Limoges *Les Oiseaux,*
adorned with colorful insects and songbirds. My contribution:
a shopping bag full of botanical shards.

Last Christmas dinner was served by my first wife
and her love on those ancient Evensongs, brought out
of the vault for good. Washing up at midnight,
my soapy fingers felt their thin misty rims at last.
I did not turn my back, and they did not hit the deck.
And when I put them away in their cupboard, I put away
as well those fifty years, all those plates and platters.

Now I dine with a woman with a wedding set of Spode
and a dishwasher. Blue and yellow birds

with fulsome tails, poised to nab
a basket of fruit. And all we use
is service for two.

HE KISSES HER AS SHE PEES

when he can catch her in the act.
Which might sound strange,
or even kinky. But when else
does just that exposure of body occur
against the enticing foil of clothes?
Flank, hip, thigh, all in a soft el,
held still for minutes at a time—
and even she'll agree, never kissed enough.

After sipping wine or tea, time always comes
for a pause, a stretch, a pee. It happens.

The girl sits, the boy kneels
and as her muscles relax
he kisses her in that pale,
blue-veined, silky fold,
that sweet declivity where leg
and middle meet. And what
could be the matter with that?

WHAT IT WAS WAS, IS THAT

I knew the struggle to be called
something other than "you guys"
in a restaurant was lost, here's when.
The young woman at Straight
Shooters Eating House in
Rawlins, Wyoming, seated us
and said with a big warm smile,
"You guys make your guys's self
comfortable."

But it's all right, I guess.
They say the language
will survive.

POWDERMILK AT THIRTY-TWO

Long may you run.

—Neil Young

Almost half my life ago, I bought
this little car. We have driven
nearly half a million miles since then.
Now the old frayed seat belt
(on a lifetime warranty!)
is being replaced at Rose Honda,
where I bought her. The frame is rusted out,
so Dave welds in a hunk of old bumper
to take the bolts. Waiting,
I sit at a picnic table behind a bank,
in the shade of a dogwood
in an ocean of asphalt
under pale blue sky and deep green firs
on the ridge behind this mall,
drinking a 24-ounce Heineken
from a brown paper bag, and ask:
what now, my old friend? When
the very wind blows through your skin
and your bones go red with rust—
what now?

THE CIRCLE

It is the unpremeditated murders you regret the most,
the witless killings that half a thought would have stayed.
The cat hit when you drove too damn fast, the wrong tree cut
when you failed to check the leaves.

"There's a black widow out here," the house painter called.
"It can't be," you said, "this side of the mountains." But it was:
come back, no doubt on your camping gear. So you caught
the spider, set up a proper habitat, named her Rosie.
I say "proper": coffee jar, screw top, twigs; a bit of sponge
for moisture. Fed her flies, and all went well—
her beautiful black shine, double-delta ruby,
virtuosic legs that caught the flies you brought
and tumbled them up in her web.
And you, ex-arachnophobe, came to love this spider.
Then, damn! Too little air, mold came, she died.
Every child knows you punch holes in the lid.

You were going to pickle Rosie for the museum. But
the spider man said, "the specimen isn't that valuable,
since it doesn't represent a local population." And
your friend asked, "She doesn't even get to join
the great circle?" So when the sun came back
and a pot of crocuses opened wide
you placed Rosie deep inside one purple cove.
Each day that crocus opened wide, you saw Rosie's
hourglass again; saw it run red into the West,
a few more times. Then that Tyrean shroud
closed up for good around her chitin form.

But wait, there's more! When you looked
next day, the pot showed only
short green stems. The yearling deer had eaten
every bloom. Sometimes the circle closes
by grace; other times by accident.

You'll take it
any way it comes.

Robert Michael Pyle's new poems are exquisitely shaped by his learned, joyful, avid consideration of the natural world and its cycles of life, death, and rebirth. Grief for his late wife, "she who made sense of the world," is balanced by all they had and did together, and what comes next. At the heart of this marvelous book is the saving grace of close observation, the life-affirming depth of feeling and engagement and understanding of birds, butterflies, fish, critters, the rich flora all around us. Pyle savors and praises, seeing what joins us to our environment and what it can show us of ourselves, lifting his and our spirits. His richly descriptive language embeds in his readers' minds such wonders as the way "the papery vanes" of butterfly wings "make hope/from nothing more than nectar and dust."

—*Floyd Skloot*

From Pangaea to pledge drives, "Pedestrains on Roadway" signs to a platypus' silky pelt, these poems cover terrain, species, and moments too often overlooked. Thankfully, Robert Michael Pyle's life work as a naturalist means he doesn't miss much, and his keen observations of the natural and human world are fully in evidence in this fine collection. Here, the reader will find poems ranging from the pleasure of pencil shavings to moving poems written for the poet's late wife Thea. Pyle's delight in language and lively wit sound clearly throughout, whether describing a Yuletide smorgasbord or his neighbors: "the Douglases, fir and squirrel; the Townsends, vole and mole." In the words of the title poem: "What gifts these are."

—*Holly Hughes*

ROBERT MICHAEL PYLE writes essay, poetry, and fiction from an old Swedish farmstead along a tributary of the Lower Columbia River in southwestern Washington. His twenty books include *Wintergreen* and *The Tangled Bank*. A Guggenheim Fellow, he has received the John Burroughs Medal and several other writing awards. Pyle's poems have appeared in magazines including the *North American Review*, and in a chapbook, *Letting the Flies Out*. *Evolution of the Genus* IRIS was his first full-length book of poems; *Chinook & Chanterelle* is his second collection from Lost Horse Press.

LOST HORSE PRESS
www.losthorsepress.org

POETRY

ISBN 978-0-9968584-0-3
$18 US